BEHIND THE WHEEL

CARS THEN AND NOW

HERE WE GO!

BEHIND THE WHEEL

CARS THEN AND NOW

Steve Otfinoski

BENCHMARK BOOKS

MARSHALL CAVENDISH
NEW YORK

Benchmark Books
Marshall Cavendish Corporation
99 White Plains Road
Tarrytown, New York 10591-9001

Library of Congress-in-Publication Data
Otfinoski, Steven.
Behind the wheel : cars then and now / by Steve Otfinoski.
    p.   cm. — (Here we go!)
Includes bibliographical references and index.
Summary: A brief overview of cars, liberally illustrated, from 1885 to the
present.
ISBN 0-7614-0403-1 (lib. bdg.)
1. Automobiles—History—Juvenile literature. [1. Automobiles—History.]
I.Title II.Series: Here we go! (New York, N.Y.)
TL147.084   1997   629.2'09—dc20   96-10861   CIP   AC

Photo research by Matthew Dudley

Cover photo: Ron Kimball

The photographs in this book are used by permission and through the cour-
tesy of: *Ron Kimball:* 6, 13, 17, 18, 19 (top and bottom), 20 (top), 20–21, 22
(top, middle, bottom), 23, 24, 25, 26, 29, 30, back cover. *The Image Bank:*
Alan Becker, 1; Eric Meola, 32. *Photo Researchers:* Tom Burnside, 2, 3, 9, 11
(bottom), 14–15; Rupert Mountain Automotive Research LTD, 3; Paolo
Koch, 11 (top); J.H. Robinson, 16. *Corbis-Bettmann:* 7, 8, 10. *Courtesy the
Behring Auto Museum, Danville CA,* 121. *Courtesy Volkswagon of America,
Inc.,* 27. *Courtesy General Motors Corporation,* 28.

Printed and bound in the United States of America

6   5   4   3   2   1

To Daniel,

who promises not to give his parents gray hairs

when he gets his driver's license

Cadillac

Cars take us wherever we want to go.
But to most people, cars are more than machines.
They are things of beauty and old friends.
The first car hit the road in 1885.
That year German inventor Karl Benz put a gasoline
engine on a tricycle and drove it through the streets
of Mannheim, Germany.
A lot has changed behind the wheel since then.

Other early cars ran on steam and electricity.
The Stanley Steamer (below) was one of the fastest and most popular cars of its day.
One steamer car, called the Wogglebug, reached a speed of over 127 miles per hour in 1906!

This electric car was quiet and easy to start.
But it could only go about twenty-five miles before needing
to be charged again.

Henry Ford made cars that most Americans could afford.
His factories turned out Model Ts by the millions.
People loved their Model Ts so much,
they called them "Tin Lizzies."

In the 1920s, young people enjoyed driving fast sports cars.

The Stutz Bearcat (above)
had huge wheels, bucket seats,
and a stripped-down body.
The Hispano-Suiza (right) had an adapted aircraft engine.
What does its back end remind you of?

Classic cars of the 1930s, like this Pierce Arrow, were streamlined for speed.

The Bugatti from France (right) was one of the decade's dream cars.

The unique shape of the radiator was modelled after a chair back designed by the carmaker's father.

13

This dazzling, cherry red Alfa Romeo from Italy was just voted the best-designed car of all time.
It was made in 1938.

The next year, World War II broke out.
Car production in much of the world came to a grinding halt.
In 1943 only 139 cars were made in all of the United States.

Carmakers turned to making trucks and tanks
and tough, little cars called "jeeps" for soldiers.
Jeeps, like the one above, could go almost anywhere,
climbing steep hills and bouncing across ditches.

After the war, Americans wanted new and better cars.
By the 1950s, young people were enjoying cars
like never before.
Teenage boys drove their dates to malt shops
and drive-in movies.
On the car radio they listened to rock and roll songs like
Chuck Berry's "Maybelline" and
the Beach Boys' "Little Deuce Coupe."
America had truly gone car crazy!

Buick Roadmaster

Corvette

Austin Healy

Thunderbird

Flashy, sleek sports cars were popular in the 1950s.
The "hottest" were convertibles.
They were fun to drive—except in the rain!

Chevrolet Bel Air

Cars grew roomier, fancier, and more comfortable.
Front grills gleamed with shiny chrome

Big fins and pointy rear lights drew
stares wherever this 1957 Cadillac went.

Red was, and still is, a "hot" car color.

The Mustang (top left) was *the* sports car of the 1960s.

It was fast and cool, but not too expensive.

The Jaguar (center) and Cobra (bottom) were also named after fast-moving animals, and for good reason.

The Volkswagen beetle from Germany (above) was slower, but it got great gas mileage.

Millions of these "bugs" roamed America's highways in the 1960s and 1970s.

Today there is a car for everyone's needs and desires—
family cars, fancy cars, sports cars, and dream cars.
The Ferrari below is one of the most expensive cars—
and one of the fastest.

Some cars of today look like cars of the future.
This one is called the Viper.
It is fast and dangerous and lies low, like the
snake it is named for.

Some cars of the future will look like cars of the past. This two-seater Plymouth Prowler is modelled after the hot rods of the 1950s.

Like Henry Ford's Model T, it will first come out in only one color—the Ford was black but this one is purple!

Here is the new Volkswagen.
It looks familiar too, but at the same time different.

This General Motors car is one of the first cars
to run on electricity in nearly a century.
Electric cars are cheap to run and don't pollute the environment.

Aviat

What kind of car do you think you'll be driving
when you're old enough to sit behind the wheel?

INDEX

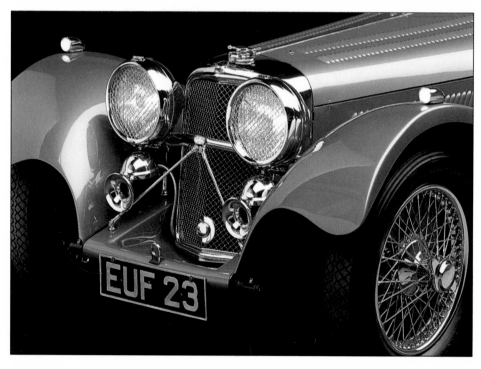

Jaguar SS-100

FIND OUT MORE

Graham, Ian. *Cars*. Chatham: NJ: Raintree Steck-Vaughn, 1993.

Johnstone, Michael. *Cars.* New York: Dorling Kindersley, 1994.

Rockwell, Anne. *Cars.* New York: Dutton Children's Books, 1984.

Struthers, John. *Dinosaur Cars: Late Great Cars from 1945 to 1966.* Minneapolis, MN: Lerner Publications, 1978.

Tessendorf, K. C. *Look Out! Here Comes the Stanley Steamer.* New York: Atheneum, 1984. Illustrated by Gloria Kamen.

STEVE OTFINOSKI has written more than sixty books for children. He also has a theater company called *History Alive!* that performs plays for schools about people and events from the past. Steve lives in Stratford, Connecticut, with his wife and two children.

DATE DUE

629.2
OTF
  Otfinoski, Steven
  Behind the wheel: cars
then and now